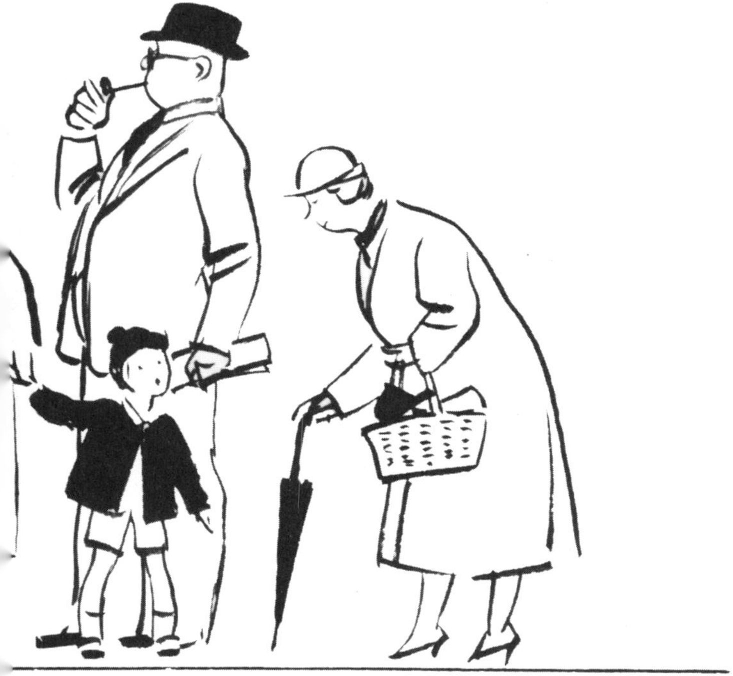

This delightful book is the latest in the series of Ladybird books that have been specially planned to help grown-ups with the world about them.

As in the other books in this series, the large, clear script, the careful choice of words, the frequent repetition and the thoughtful matching of text with pictures all enable grown-ups to think they have taught themselves to cope. The subject of the book will greatly appeal to grown-ups.

Series 999

THE LADYBIRD
BOOKS FOR GROWN-UPS SERIES

THE MID-LIFE CRISIS

by

J. A. HAZELEY, N.S.F.W. and J. P. MORRIS, O.M.G.

(Authors of '1,000 Films To Fall Asleep In Before You Die')

Publishers: Ladybird Books Ltd, Loughborough
Printed in England. If wet, Italy.

When we are young, we all dream of doing something wonderful and exciting with our lives.

What will we be? A cosmonaut? An underwater detective? A tommy gunner? A groin surgeon?

Anything is possible.

And then, one day, it isn't.

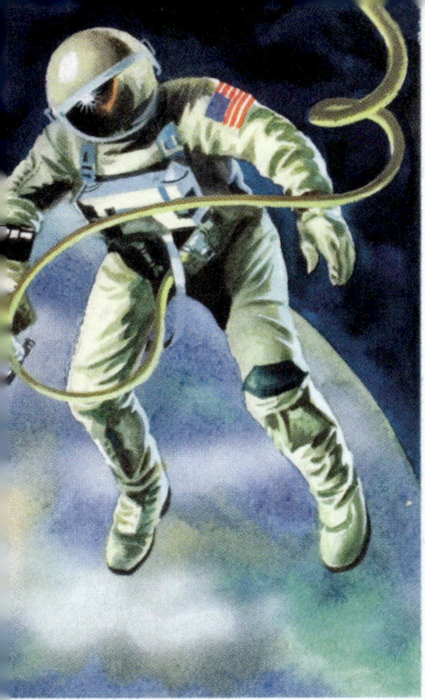
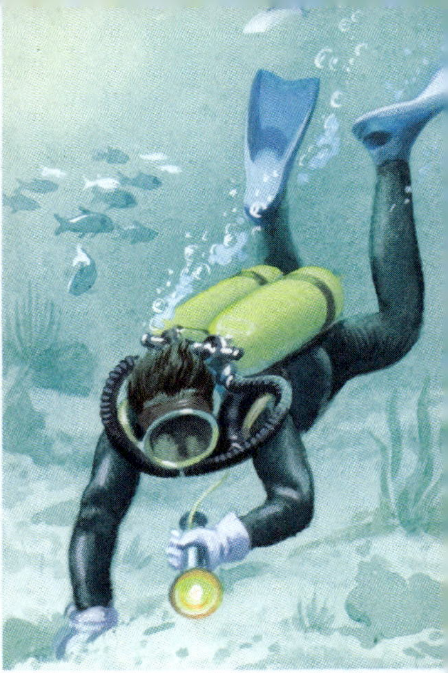
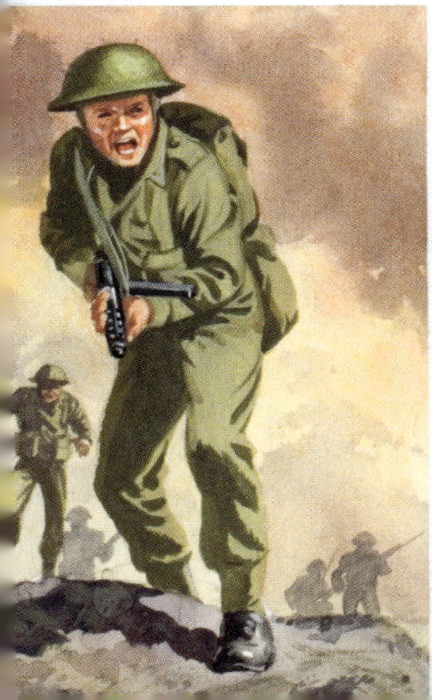
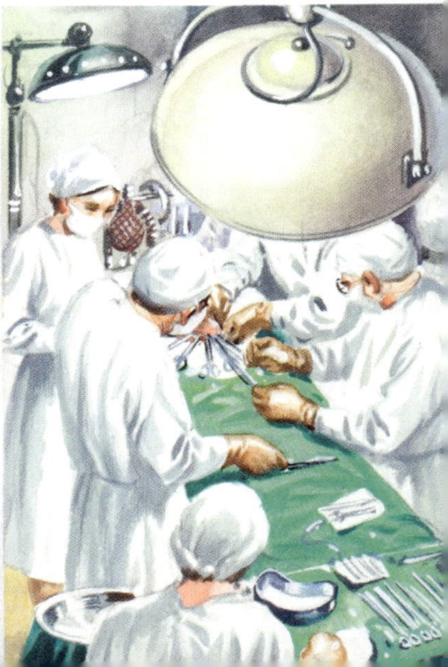

Jason's mid-life crisis started one Sunday morning in B&Q when he spotted a tub of boat varnish.

"I will never own a boat," he thought to himself.

Jason has never wanted to own a boat. But now, not owning one is all he can think about.

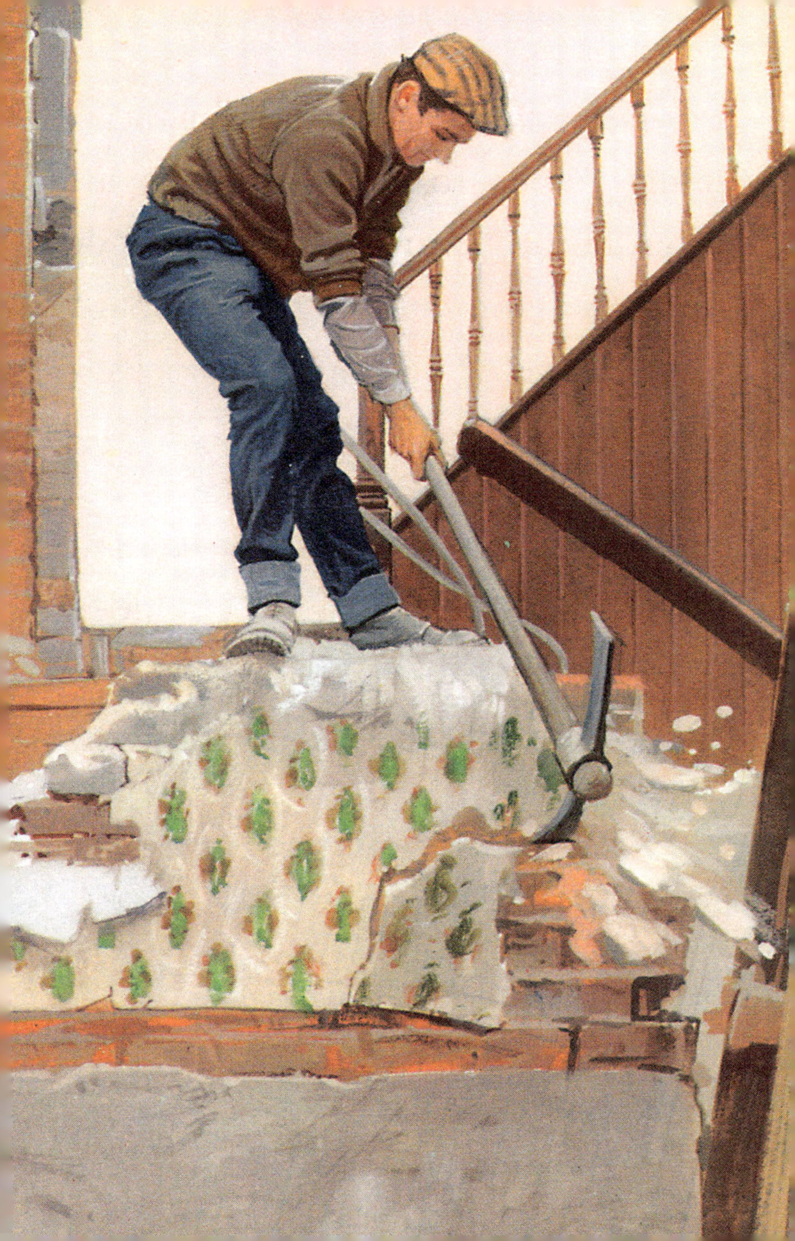

Gwen has a 2:1 in Ancient History. She always planned to write a series of novels about Boadicea.

Gwen is covered in apple sauce and has spent this afternoon clapping.

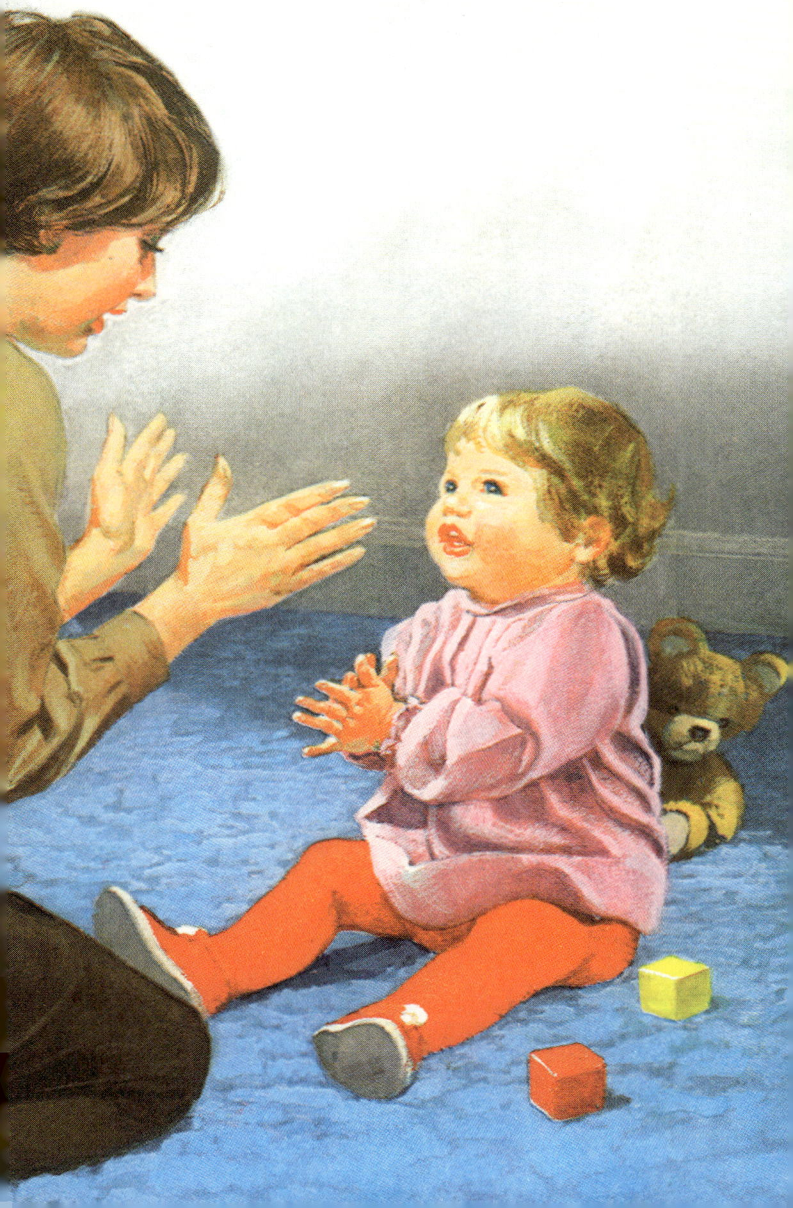

Jeff did not think of himself as having a mid-life crisis until he realised that the people starting university this year were born when he was twenty-five.

Jeff has come to the Arctic Circle to hunt and kill a whale.

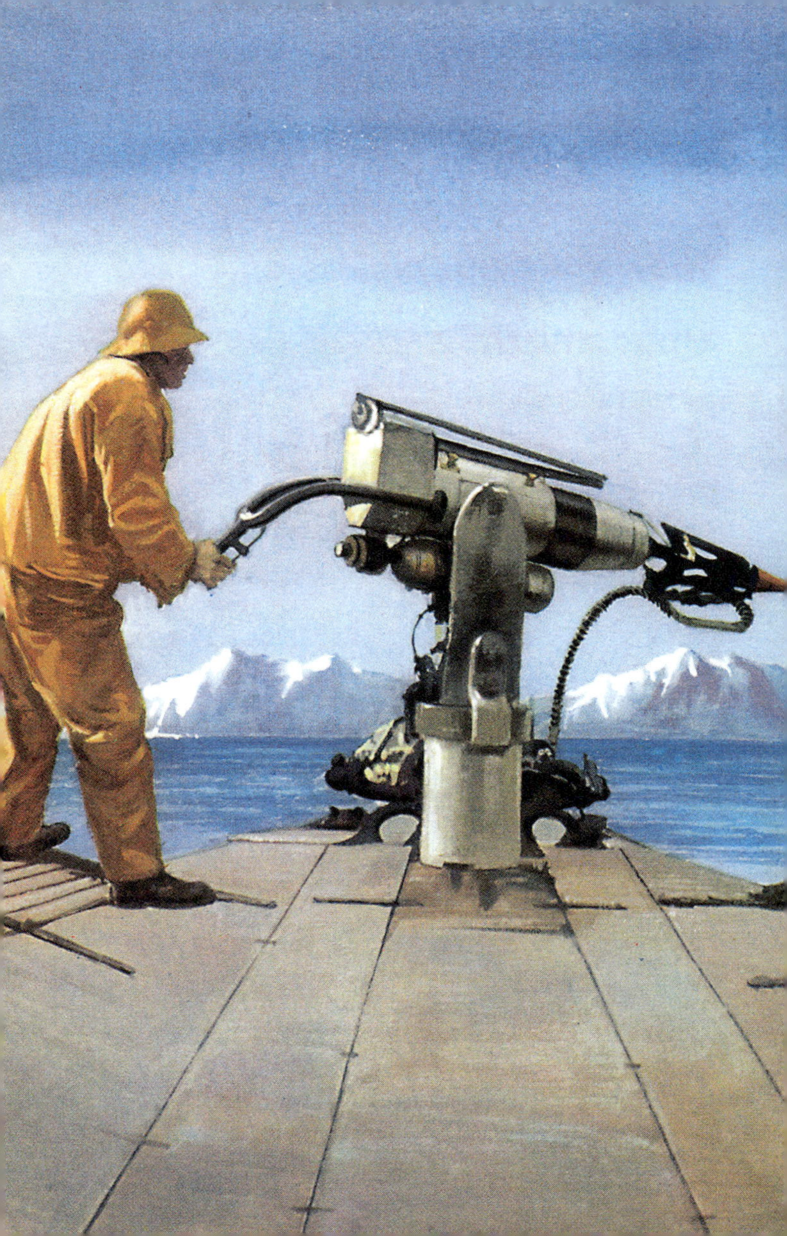

Mid-lifers like to count how fast time is passing because it helps them to panic.

"It's incredible," says Vivian. "The gap between now and the first Beastie Boys album is roughly the same as the gap between that album and Elvis's first LP."

"Help me, please," sobs Vivian. "Somebody make it stop."

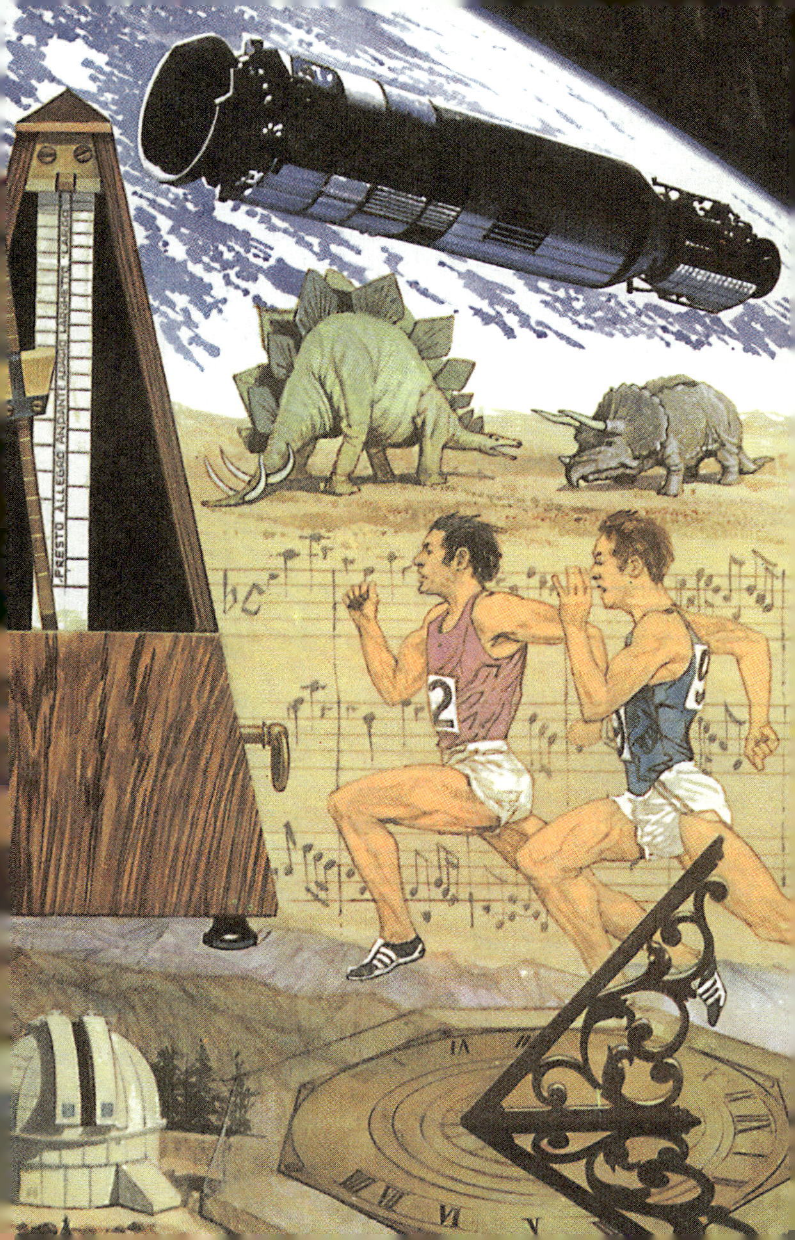
PRESTO ALLEGRO ANDANTE ADAGIO LARGHETTO LARGO

Joe's body used to agree with him.

It used to agree that his shirt fitted, that he could manage another pint, that he would be awake when the train reached his station, and that he had finished weeing.

Now Joe's body disagrees with him on all these things.

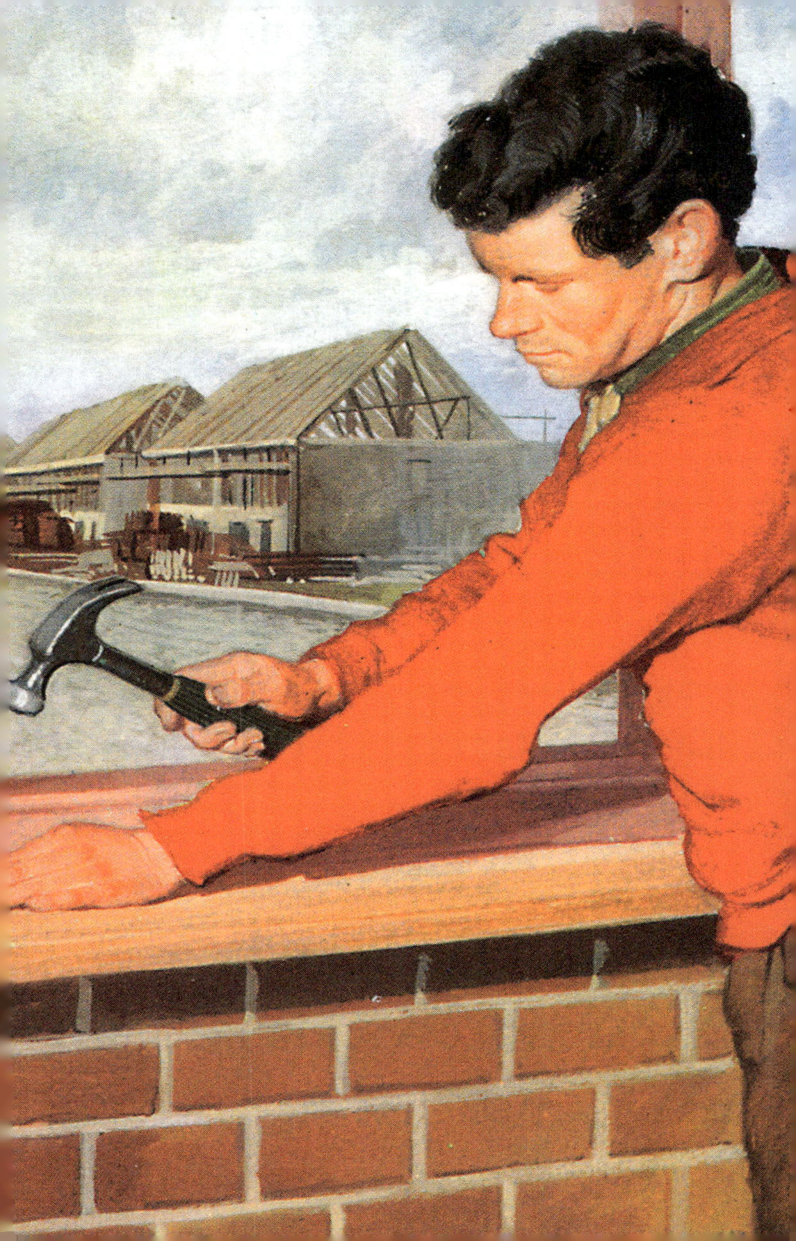

Philip has a recurring dream where he is an overstuffed dummy on a blazing bonfire. Children point at him and laugh.

"Look at him," they say. "He is fat and hopeless."

"Burn him! That's all he's good for! At least he can keep us warm!"

Philip does not burn. He cannot even do that properly.

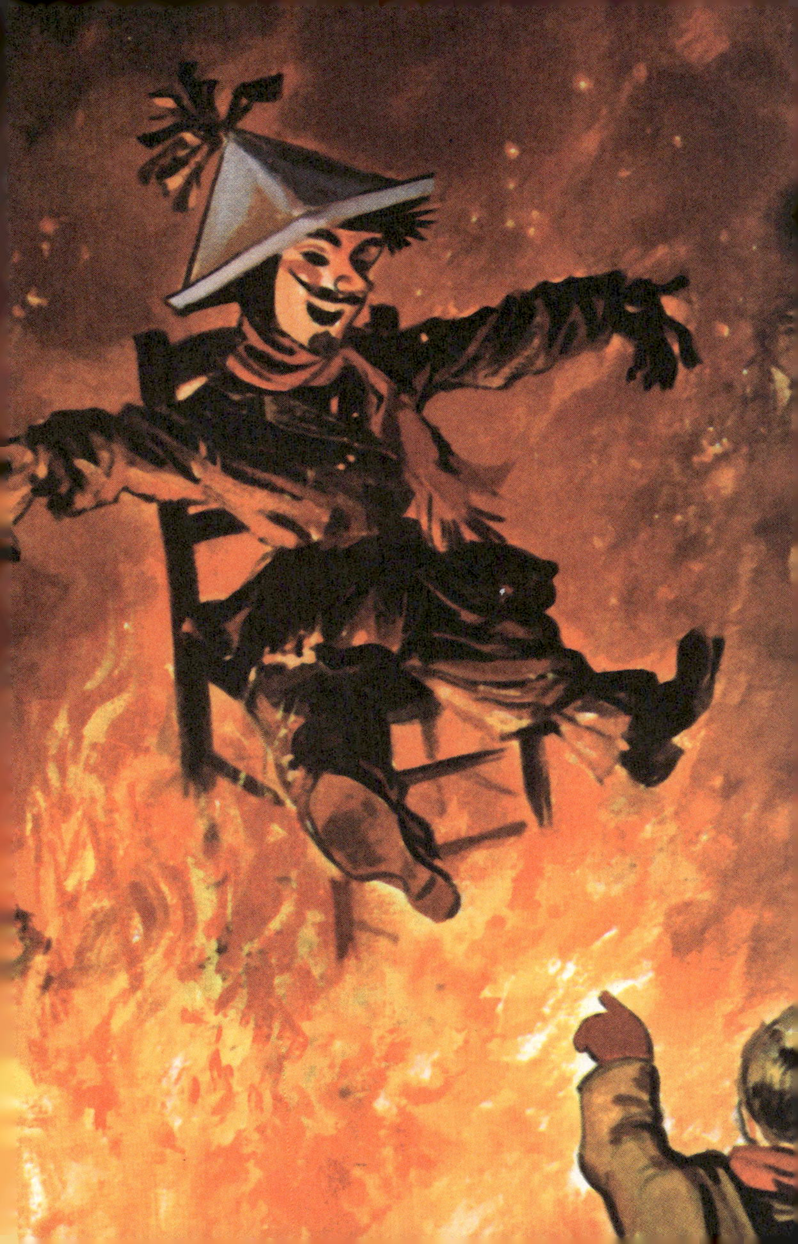

After his divorce, Nick sold his sensible car and bought a coupé.

In ten years' time, Nick will look back at pictures of himself and "The Lady" and realise that he looked an astonishing knob.

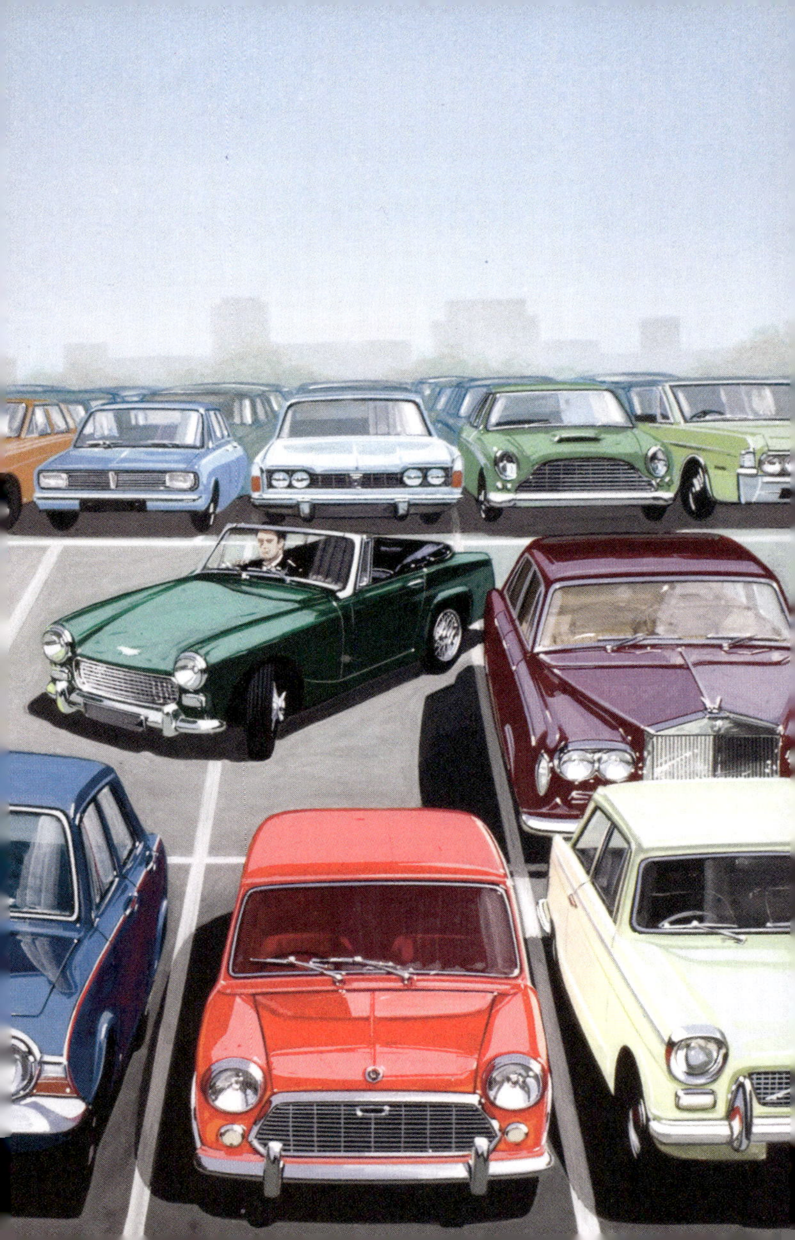

In a war, people do not have mid-life crises. They are much too grateful to be alive.

At this airfield, mid-lifers can have a wartime fantasy day. They can fly a Spitfire, and even do a loop-the-loop.

For an extra fee, they can be shot down by authentic Luftwaffe aircraft, and killed.

Many people find this helps.

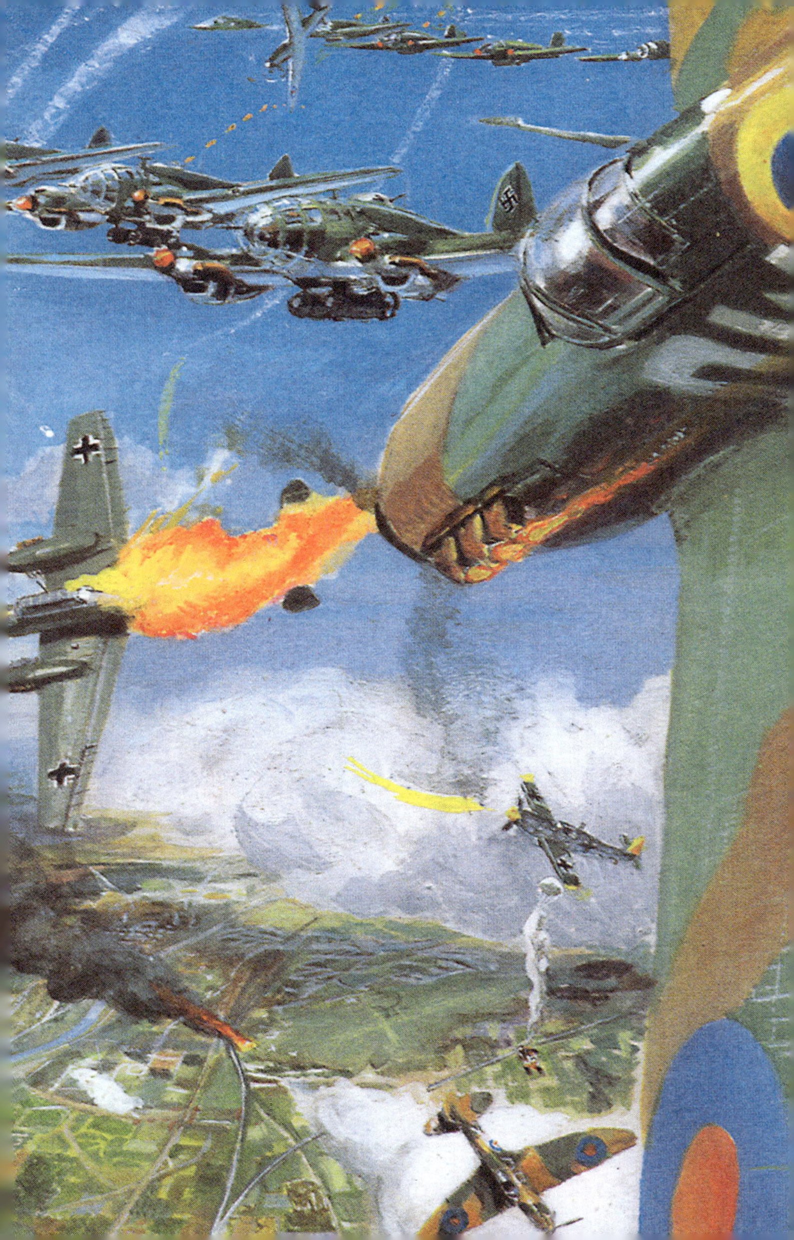

Phil does not regret leaving his wife, growing his hair and starting to wear cowboy boots.

If he had not done that, he would never have met Megan.

As long as Phil avoids making cultural references from before 1990, never reveals he has a blueyonder e-mail address and tries not to have a heart attack, he and Megan have a great future.

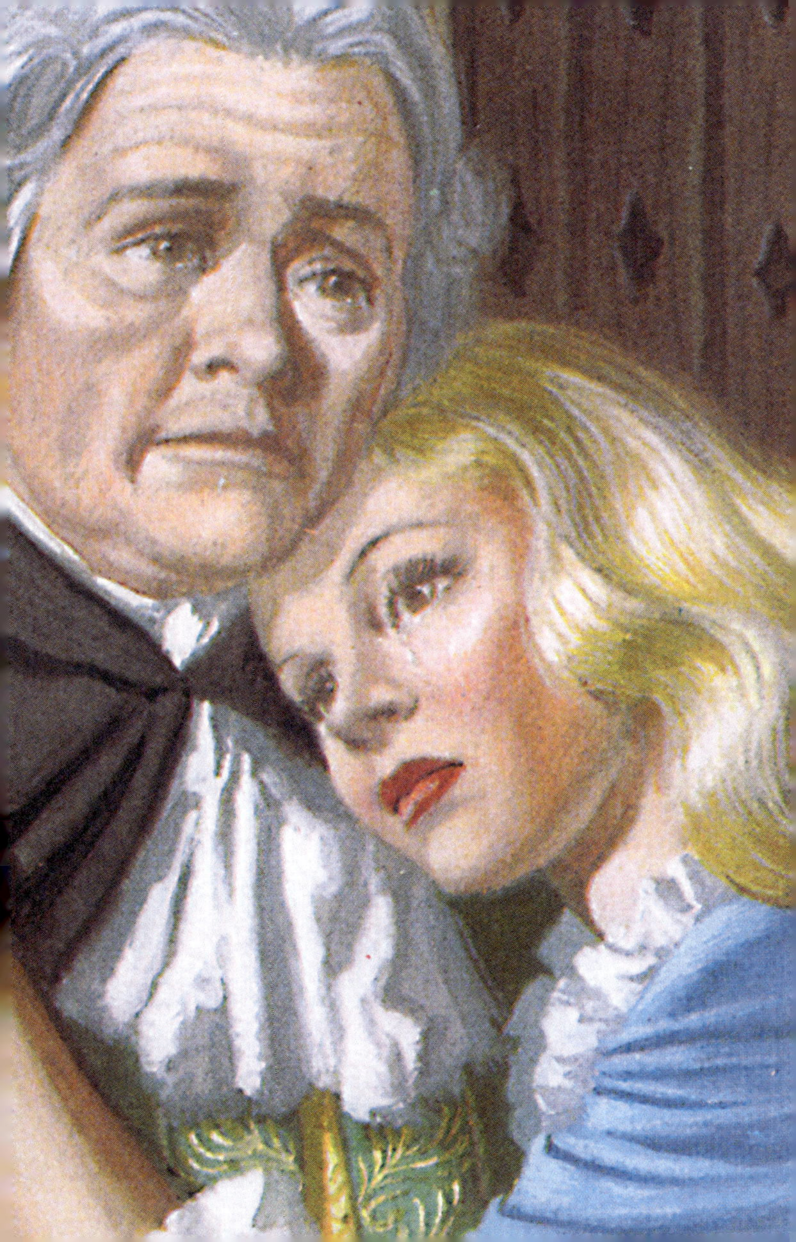

Growing up brings responsibility. For example, having a family to support can be very expensive.

Fortunately, by mid-life, most people find they are earning a little more money than they did when they were younger.

Which can also be spent on bigger versions of all the toys they wanted when they were six.

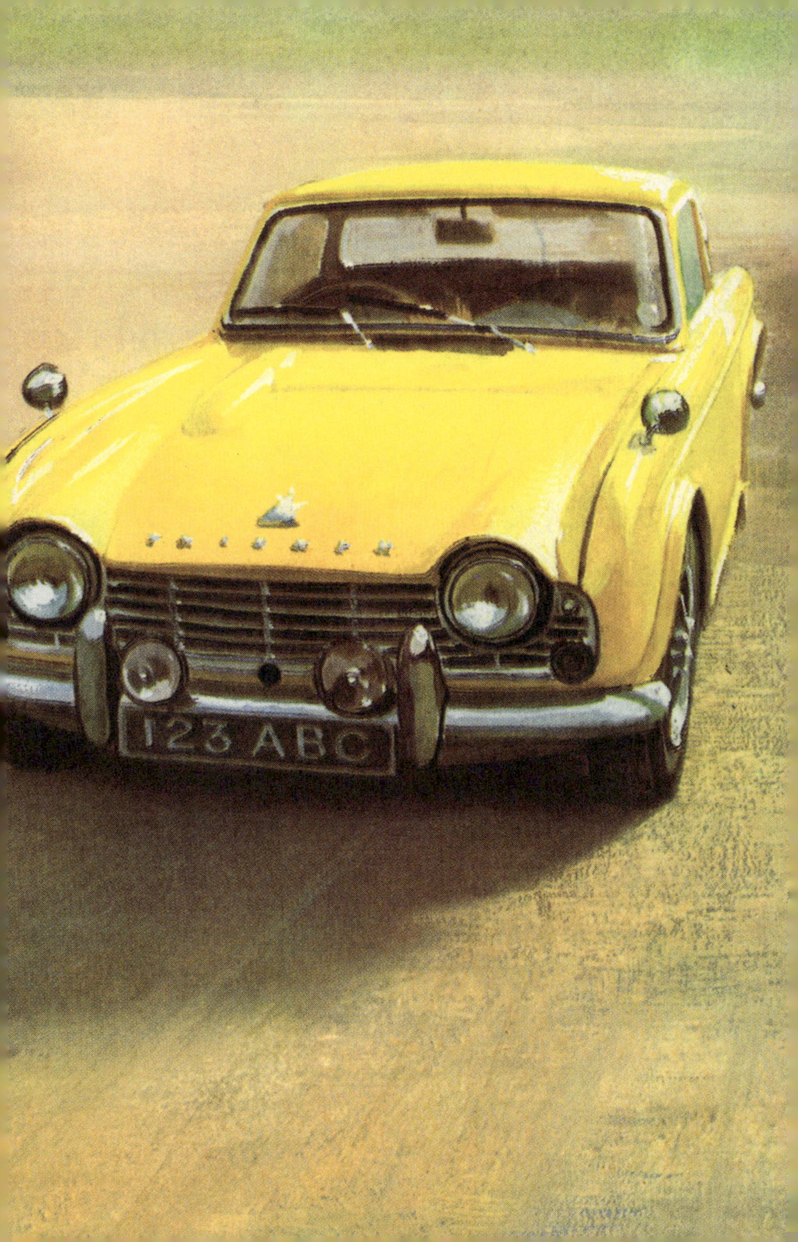
123 ABC

Kathy's youngest left home last year. Kathy has more time for herself now, to see old friends. A friend came round with some old school photographs.

"I was beautiful," thought Kathy to herself, when she saw the pictures. "Nobody said."

Kathy has started an affair with the man at the cooker showroom.

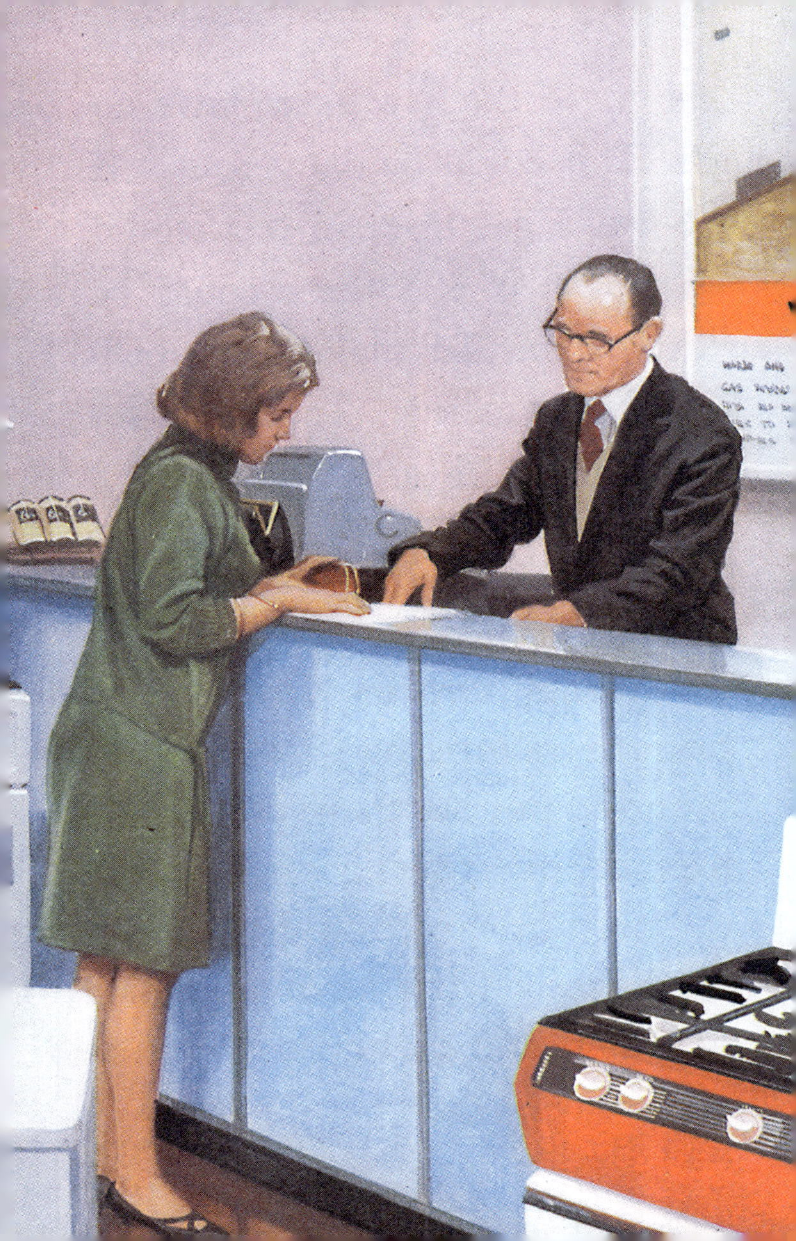

Frank is forty-one. He has been to a record shop. He has re-bought all the music he liked when he was young, but on the most inconvenient possible format.

He also asked the twenty-two-year-old behind the counter what new records were good. He bought everything she recommended because she had amazing hair.

He hates all the new records, but not as much as he hates himself.

ALLR 801

HI FIDELITY

Paul recently bought a shark-tooth necklace. Ray has spent the morning bidding on a leather biker jacket. Last night, Charlie Googled local triathlons.

They are now talking about cutting their family holidays short next year, and going to Glastonbury together instead.

"We could lie and say it's a conference," says Ray.

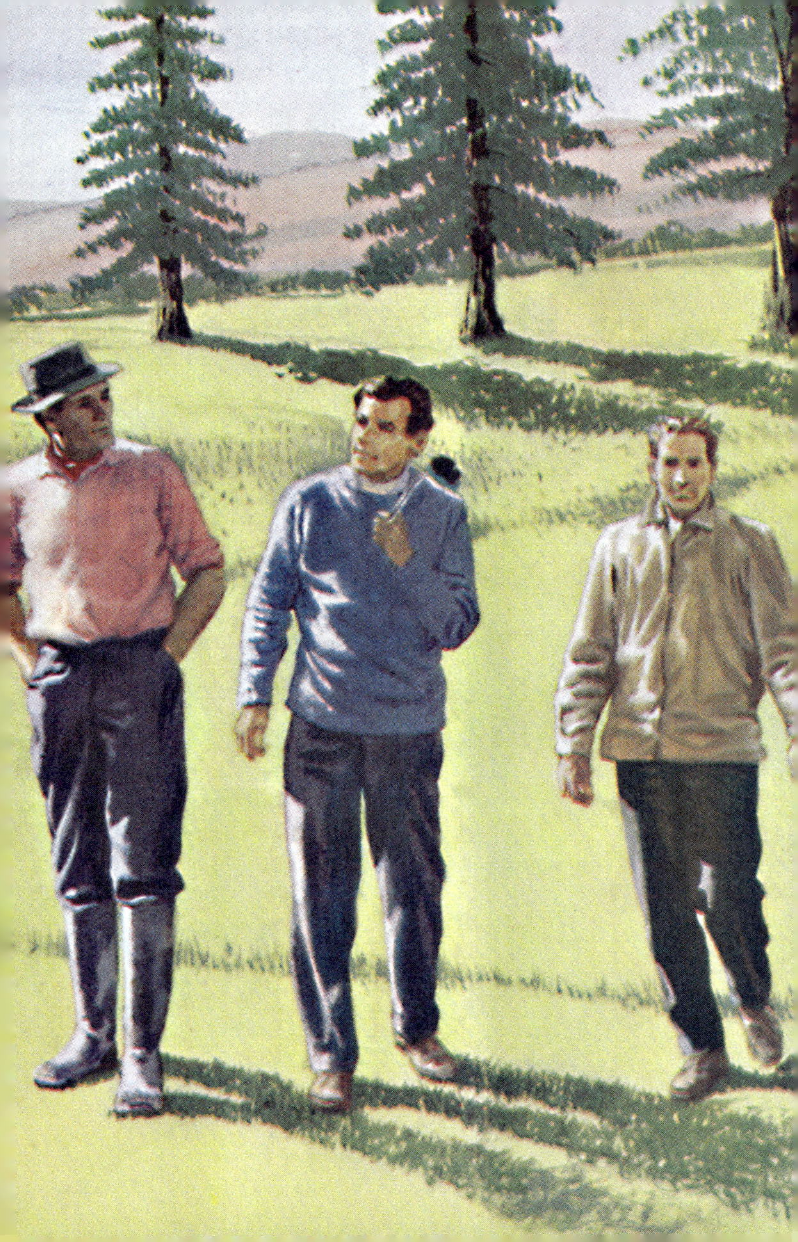

Sally has tried lots of things to make herself feel younger: running, glamping, Pilates, adult colouring books, a "mummy make-over," Bikram planking, Platonic irrigation and having an inappropriate relationship with a rangy twenty-something intern called Zeb, who has three beards and a Lego earring.

Sally has given up and is now thinking of joining the National Trust.

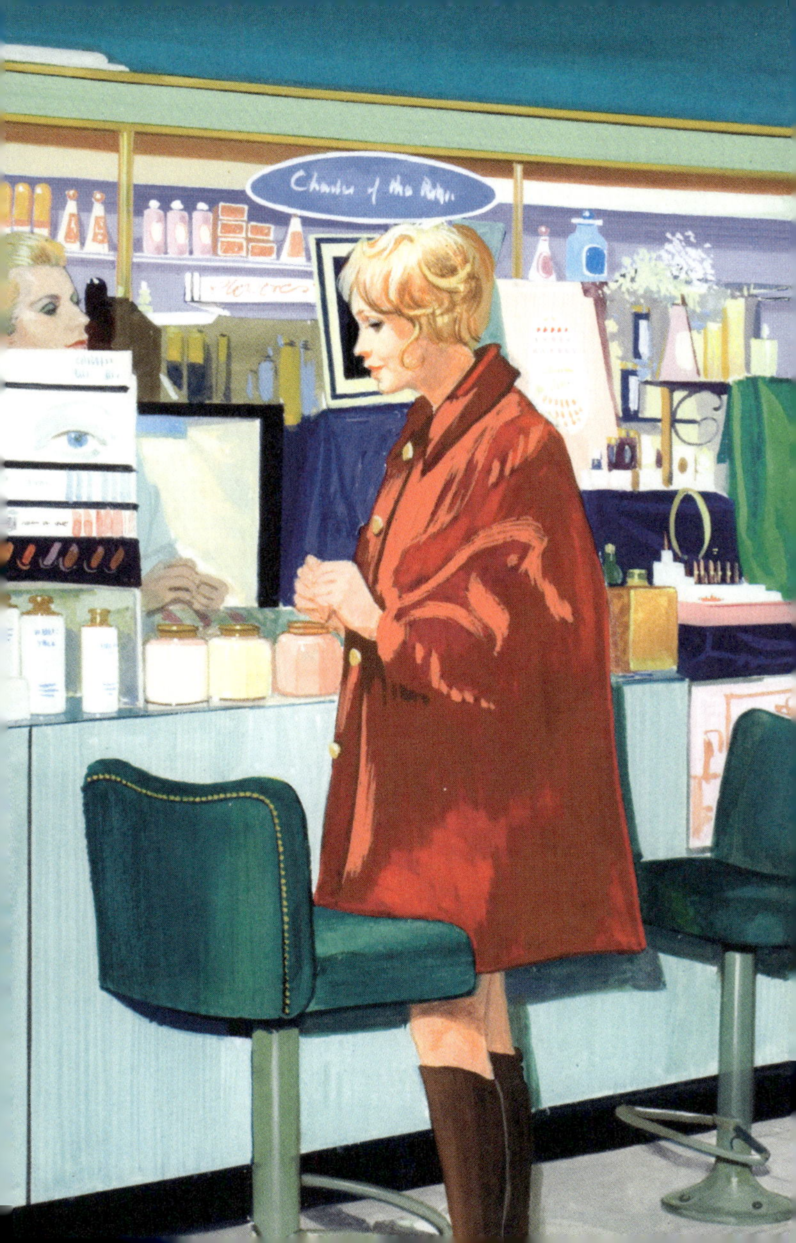

Duncan bought a second-hand bicycle using money he got for his thirty-eighth birthday.

Three years later, Duncan is competing in the Tour de France on a bike that cost more than the deposit for his first flat.

Duncan has forgotten what he is trying to prove.

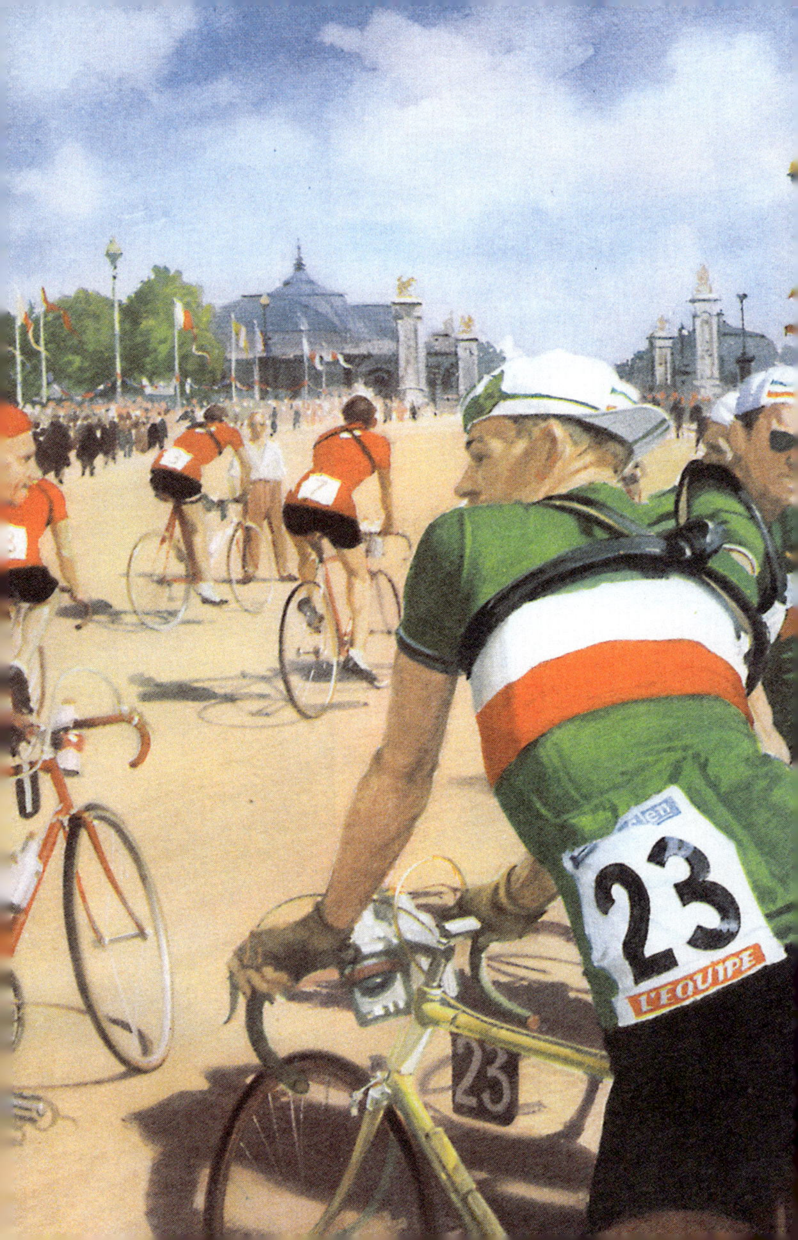
23
L'EQUIPE
23

Tom is fed up. The band he was in at college played a reunion show at the football club bar last week and they were rubbish.

The evening cost him over £140 in drinks, taxis and babysitters.

Tom has now put his Les Paul copy guitar on eBay.

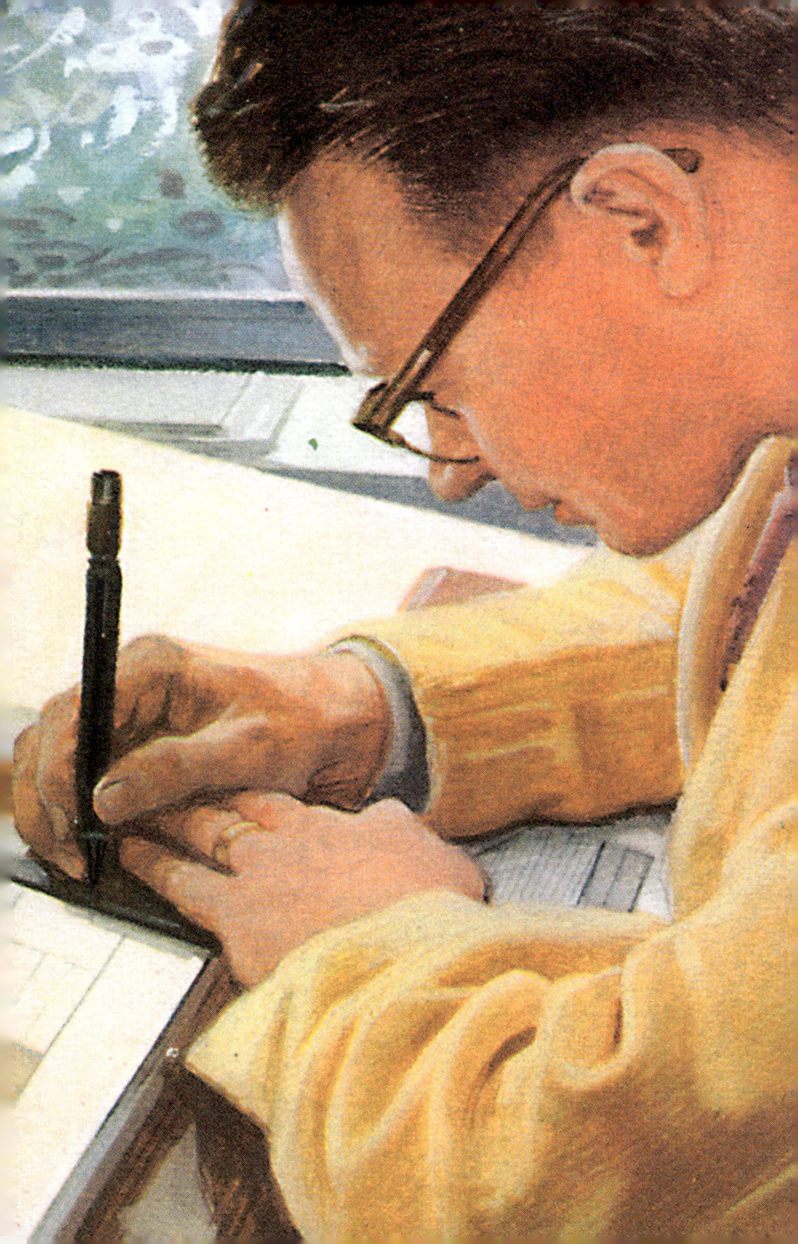

Gerry is explaining his wishes to his barber. Gerry's cut involves layers, dyes and four separate thickening products. But it is worth it.

In the end, Gerry will have a full head of hair, if viewed face-on, and not from behind or above, out of direct sunlight and away from high winds.

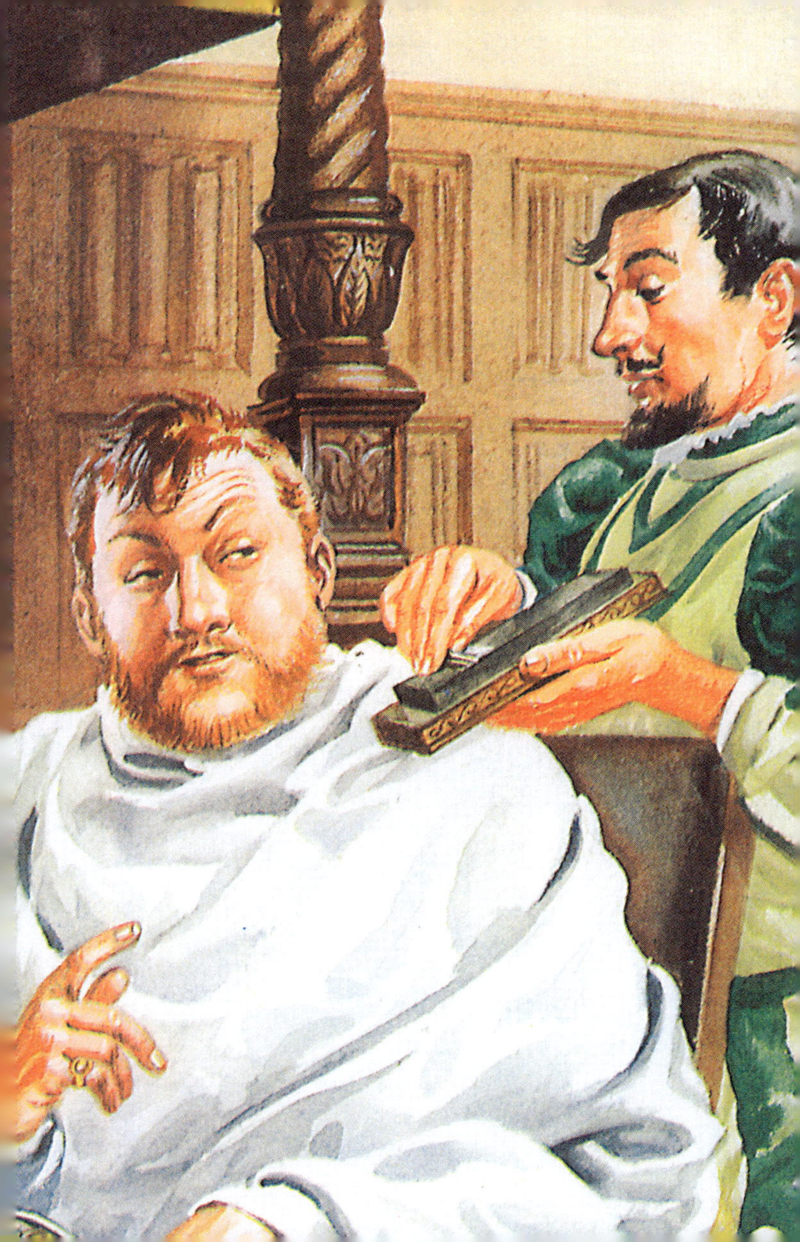

Mark's partner, Trina, has just called to say the PTA meeting is running late.

"Eat without me," she says.

Mark rings off quickly. He feels guilty, even though Trina cannot possibly know he has spent the last three hours on Facebook looking for old photos of girls he was at school with.

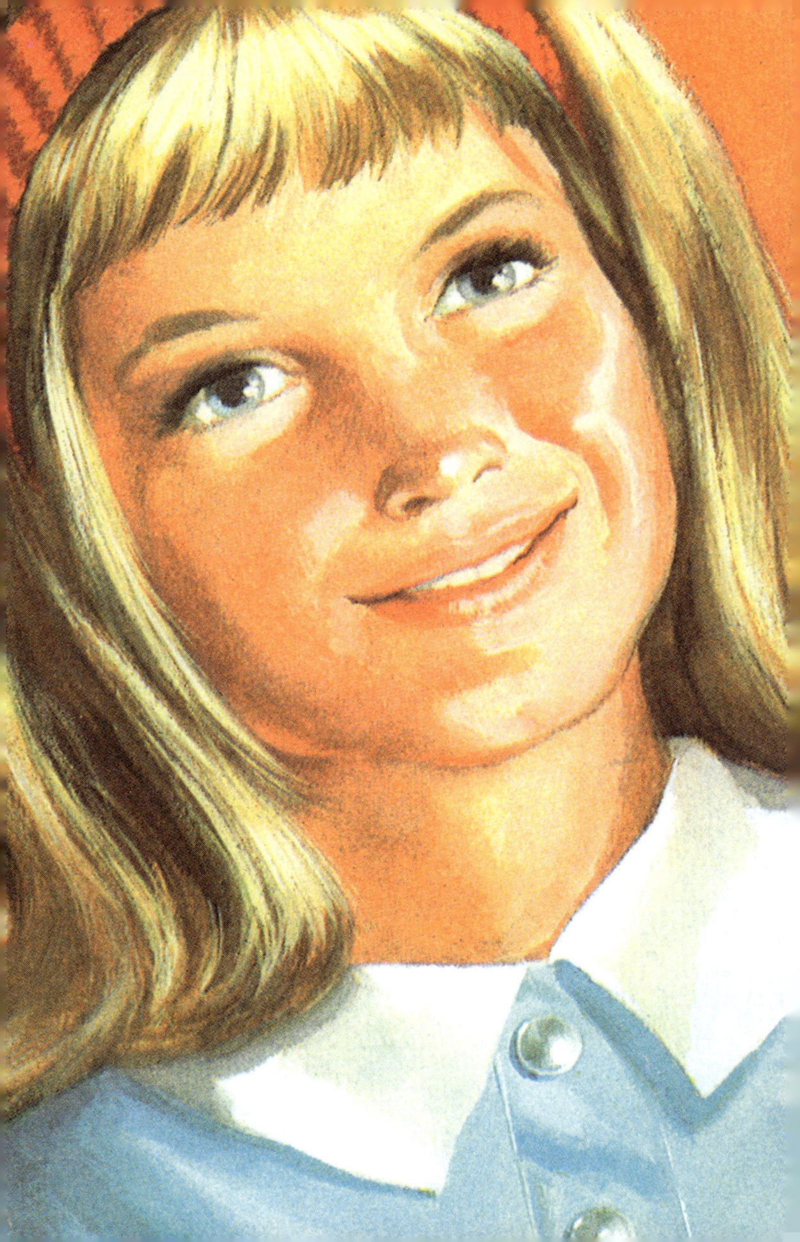

Suzy is at the hairdresser's.

She wants to look good because tonight she is going to a gabba all-nighter under a railway arch with her estranged daughter.

"Dye it blue, please," says Suzy.

Suzy is wondering which bra will best show off her new tattoo.

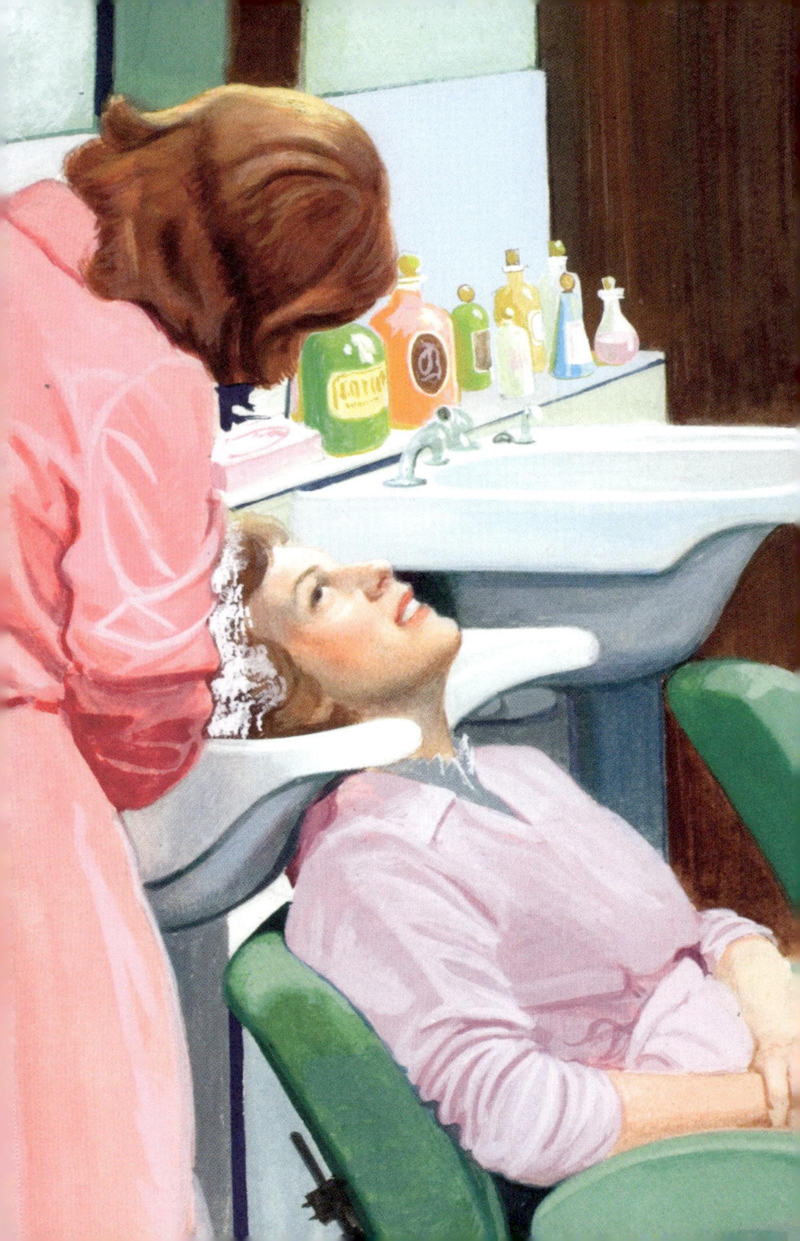

On the way back from this lads' weekend, Jim will be cautioned at Schiphol airport for possession of marijuana.

The two police officers will be half his age.

It will be the first marijuana Jim has possessed in two decades.

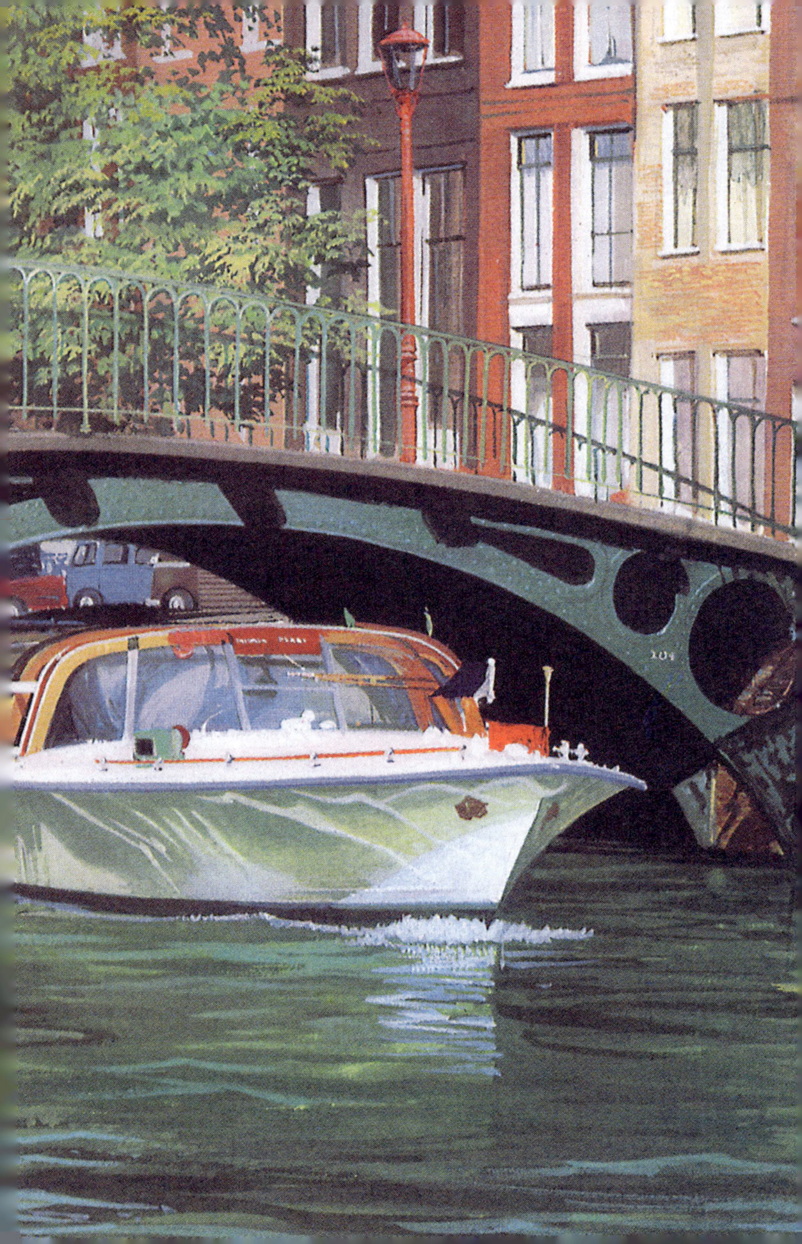

Amanda is forty and childless. She spends most of her evenings at bars and clubs, meeting people who are ten years younger than her and applying lots of forgiving filters to photos of herself she posts on Instagram.

Soon she will buy a cat.

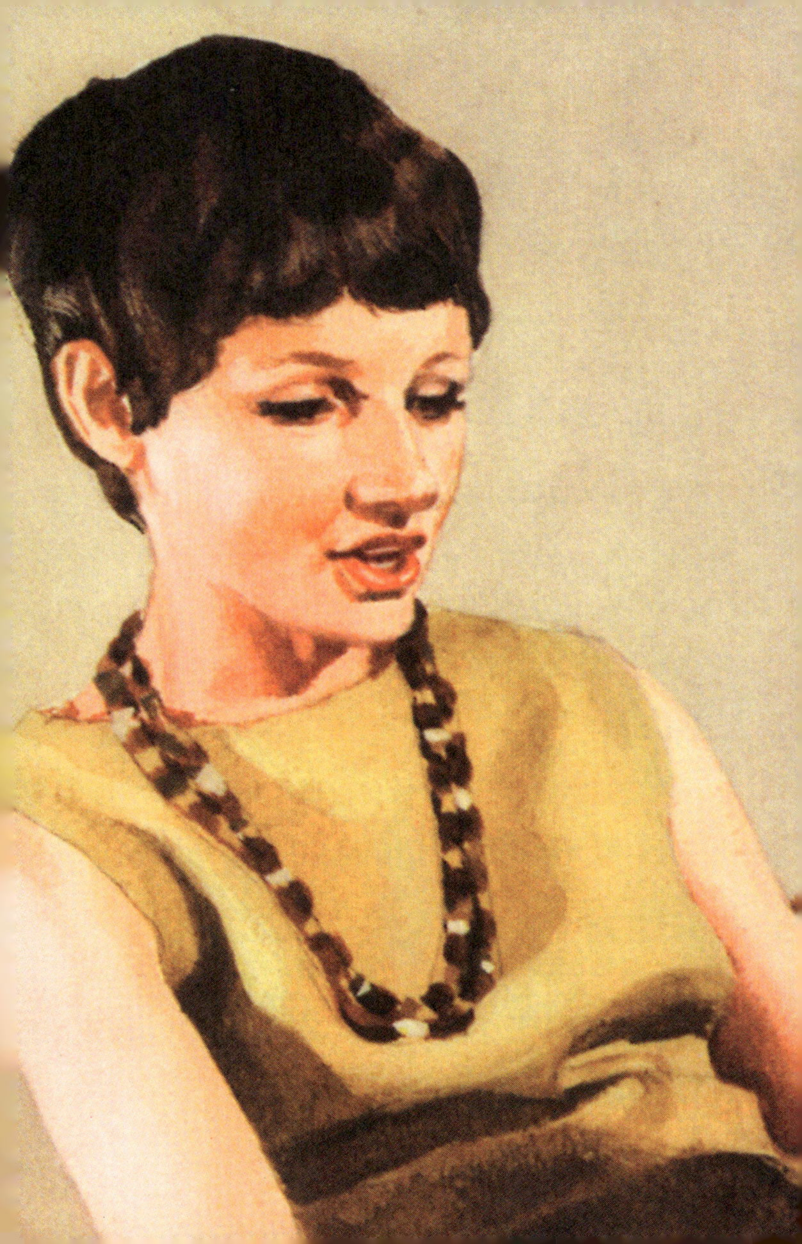

Brendan is exhausted. Today he has run four miles in his new vintage Dunlop Green Flash trainers, cycled ten miles, done a Zumba class, flirted with his PA and spent the evening looking up various aches and lumps on the Internet in case they are early signs of cancer or diabetes.

He will sleep until 3 a.m. when he will be woken by anxiety dreams about a twenty-three-year-old graduate who can do almost everything he does for half the money.

Colin spent his redundancy money on the loudest motorcycle he could find.

He has stopped at a petrol station on the way to an archive where he is researching his family tree.

"You only live once," Colin says with a wink to the girl on the moped.

The girl smiles back at him. Colin reminds her of her dad.

THE AUTHORS would like to record their gratitude and offer their apologies to the many Ladybird artists whose luminous work formed the glorious wallpaper of countless childhoods. Revisiting it for this book as grown-ups has been a privilege.

MICHAEL JOSEPH

UK | USA | Canada | Ireland | Australia
India | New Zealand | South Africa

Michael Joseph is part of the Penguin Random House group of companies whose addresses can be found at global.penguinrandomhouse.com

Penguin Random House UK

First published 2015
015

Text copyright © Jason Hazeley and Joel Morris, 2015
All images copyright © Ladybird Books Ltd, 2015

The moral right of the authors has been asserted

Printed in Italy by L.E.G.O. S.p.A

A CIP catalogue record for this book is available from the British Library

ISBN: 978–0–718–18353–0

www.greenpenguin.co.uk

MIX
Paper from responsible sources
FSC® C018179
www.fsc.org

Penguin Random House is committed to a sustainable future for our business, our readers and our planet. This book is made from Forest Stewardship Council® certified paper.